TILLIE PIERCE'S CIVIL WAR STORY

KATIE MARSICO
ILLUSTRATED BY THOMAS GIRARD

Lerner Publications ◆ Minneapolis

PUBLISHER'S NOTE

This story is based on historical events. The people, places, and dates are known through primary source accounts of the time. While inspired by known facts, dialogue and some descriptive details have been fictionalized.

To my mom, Ann Konrath, who has done more than her fair share of unexpected nursing and who has always demonstrated exceeding compassion to anyone she has comforted

Lerner Publications Company
A division of Lerner Publishing Group, Inc.
241 First Avenue North
Minneapolis, MN 55401 USA

For reading levels and more information, look up this title at www.lernerbooks.com.

The images in this book are used with the permission of: Library of Congress (LC-DIG-pga-02102), p. 30; Library of Congress (pa0021), p. 31.

Main body text set in Rotis Serif Std 55 Regular 15/24.
Typeface provided by Adobe Systems.

Library of Congress Cataloging-in-Publication Data

Names: Marsico, Katie, 1980– author.
Title: Tillie Pierce's Civil War story / by Katie Marsico.
Description: Minneapolis : Lerner Publications, [2018] | Series: Narrative nonfiction: kids in war | Includes bibliographical references. | Audience: 7–10. | Audience: K–3.
Identifiers: LCCN 2017010168 (print) | LCCN 2017012813 (ebook) | ISBN 9781512497861 (eb pdf) | ISBN 9781512456776 (lb : alk. paper)
Subjects: LCSH: Alleman, Tillie Pierce—Juvenile literature. | Gettysburg, Battle of, Gettysburg, Pa., 1863—Juvenile literature.
Classification: LCC E475.53 (ebook) | LCC E475.53 .M34 2018 (print) | DDC 973.7/349—dc23

LC record available at https://lccn.loc.gov/2017010168

Manufactured in the United States of America
1-42946-26762-9/21/2017

FOREWORD

From 1861 to 1865, the Civil War divided the United States. Several Southern states broke apart from the rest of the nation and formed the Confederate States of America, or the Confederacy. The rest of the nation was known as the Union.

In June of 1863, Confederate forces marched through Gettysburg, Pennsylvania. They raided the town for supplies. Union troops were not far behind them, and the Battle of Gettysburg raged from July 1 to 3.

During the battle, fifteen-year-old Tillie Pierce stayed with the Weikert family in the country, a few miles south of Gettysburg. Tillie's parents thought she would be safer away from the action. Little did they know how close she would be.

JULY 2, 1863, THE WEIKERT FARM

The scorching July sun beat down on miles of grain fields, meadows, and fruit orchards. As Tillie Pierce moved across the yard, she raised one hand to shade her eyes. In her other hand, she carried a tin cup brimming with cool water.

The thick grass around Tillie was filled with Union soldiers in their blue uniforms. Many wore slings and bandages. Little by little, Tillie was growing used to the sight of such injuries. The Battle of Gettysburg had begun just one day earlier, but bruised and bloody Union soldiers had quickly appeared across the farm.

The Weikerts made space for the soldiers in their home, barn, and carriage house. In the basement kitchen, Mrs. Weikert always seemed to be stirring broth or shoveling dough into the oven. Along with the Weikerts' daughters, Tillie handed out meals to the soldiers who were well enough to eat. She also brought water to passing troops on the road.

"Here you are, sir," said Tillie. She handed the drink to a soldier who had been asking for water. A wrapping barely covered the wound on his head, and a deep cut ran close to his eye.

"Thank you kindly, miss," the soldier told Tillie in a cracked, raspy voice. He nodded at her before draining the cup.

"No trouble," replied Tillie. She smiled at the man and the small cluster of soldiers standing near him. "Have you eaten? If you'd like, I can bring you a loaf of fresh bread to share. There's some broth too."

"Please!" the soldiers said eagerly. They sounded as if she had promised them a huge feast. Tillie wished she had more to offer. Yet she hoped she was bringing the soldiers some comfort, even as the war raged around them.

FROM FARMHOUSE TO HOSPITAL

"May I have more food, Mrs. Weikert?" Tillie called out as she headed back into the basement. She looked around and realized how cramped the room was becoming. Yesterday there had been far fewer soldiers. Today the wounded seemed to be filling the Weikerts' property

at a much faster pace. The gunshots
in the distance seemed to be growing
louder as well.

"Right away," replied Mrs. Weikert.
She arranged the bread and broth on a
serving platter. "Be careful though, my
dear. Our officers are doing their best
to track the Confederates' position. But
all the same, watch yourself."

"Of course," Tillie said as she trekked back into the midday heat. Despite Mrs. Weikert's warning, her mood lightened for just a moment. Feeding the Union troops helped take her mind off the terrible situation around her. Besides, the men were so grateful that Tillie truly enjoyed her job.

But as Tillie rounded the corner of the Weikerts' stone house, her smile vanished. She dropped the platter she was carrying. A small group of soldiers was sprawled in a heap on the ground. None of the soldiers were moving.

Tillie shivered. Her feet felt stuck
to the grass, as if they were too heavy
to lift. Then she spied a pool of blood
slowly forming around the bodies.
With her heart pounding, Tillie turned
and ran.

UNDER ATTACK

"They're dead," Tillie stammered
as she sped back into the Weikerts'
basement. "The soldiers that were
standing along the wall. I have
no idea what happened. I was just
bringing out more food . . ." Two
officers who were reviewing a map
in a far corner of the room leaped up
and raced past her. Mrs. Weikert came
over and took her hands.

"Stay indoors," she told Tillie.
Then Mrs. Weikert looked around at
her daughters. "All of you. Until we
know what happened." The Weikert
girls nodded silently. A few minutes
later, one of the officers reappeared.
Mr. Weikert was with him.

"Your farm is in the direct line of fire, ma'am," the officer told Mrs. Weikert. "They shot at our men from the hills." Tillie gripped the edge of the table and tried to steady herself. How was that possible? She had just been speaking to them!

"We've tried to shelter the wounded indoors," continued the officer. "But from the look of things, I'm afraid conditions are getting cramped." Mrs. Weikert started to reply, but her voice was drowned out by a deafening roar.

The ceiling shook violently. Iron
pots and pans hanging from the walls
crashed down. Tillie crouched on
the floor and covered her head. Her
ears rang.

"Confederate cannons," shouted the officer to Mr. and Mrs. Weikert. He walked briskly toward the door. "We'll hear more of that cannon fire. I expect your farm will soon be bursting at the seams with soldiers."

A NEW UNION NURSE

By the following day, Tillie learned
how right the officer had been.
Confederate cannons continued to
blast, and more soldiers flooded the
farm. The moans of men in pain
became louder. Union soldiers carried
the wounded in on stretchers or slung
them across their backs.

Meanwhile, Tillie and the Weikerts tore linen and clothing into bandage strips. They also helped doctors treat the soldiers. Sometimes Tillie's hands trembled as she prepared to assist the surgeons. She was tired and nervous— and she wasn't a trained nurse.

"I *must*," Tillie would think to herself. "I owe it to the men in my care." She repeated the words in her mind as the sounds of battle grew softer on July 3. She was tired, but she knew her work was far from over. Tillie was working in the basement. While she held up a wounded soldier's elbow, a doctor wound a linen bandage around his shoulder.

"The bullet is out," the doctor announced. "There's no sign of infection either, so I'm not worried you'll lose your arm. That's a blessing, lad."

Tillie swallowed hard and looked away. She knew the doctor wasn't exaggerating.

"Once I tie the ends of this bandage together, gently lower his arm," the doctor told Tillie. When he had finished, the doctor cleaned his hands in a basin of water. "Can you bring him some food? It will help him regain his strength."

"Yes, sir," Tillie assured the doctor as he moved on to his next patient. She turned to face the soldier. "I'll be right back. I'm sure Mrs. Weikert already has a meal waiting for you."

A WORLD CHANGED BY WAR

Tillie slowly raised a spoon of broth to the man's lips. "Do you feel well enough to eat?" she asked.

"Indeed," the soldier answered. He was pale, but his cheeks regained some color at the sight of food. "It's been a while since I've had anything home-cooked."

"Have you been fighting that long?" Tillie wondered. "Were you in town at all?"

"It's bad all around Gettysburg," the soldier noted. "In town. Throughout the countryside. Buildings and fields are burning, and there are bodies everywhere." The soldier paused. "Word is that we've beaten the Confederates. Like we've never beaten them before. It's just that . . . well, if it's true, victory came at a high price."

"You're right," whispered Tillie as she stared at the floor. "I don't know where my family is now. I don't know if they survived. It's been a horrible three days. The world is different." She breathed in and finally looked up again. To her surprise, the soldier was smiling.

"Not all the world is different," he said. "Some folks are just as kind as they always were." Tillie hoped the soldier was right. If he was, perhaps the Battle of Gettysburg hadn't destroyed *everything.*

AFTERWORD

About fifty-one thousand Union and Confederate soldiers were injured, killed, captured, or reported missing during the Battle of Gettysburg. It was among the bloodiest battles of the Civil War. Yet it was also a turning point. The Confederacy never fully recovered after this failed invasion of the North. In 1865 Union forces won the Civil War.

Following the Battle of Gettysburg, Tillie was reunited with her family. Later, she wrote about her experiences in a book that was published in 1889. She died in Philadelphia, Pennsylvania, in 1914.

March 11, 1848 Tillie Pierce is born in
Gettysburg, Pennsylvania.

December 20, 1860 South Carolina leaves the
Union. Over the next few months, ten other
Southern states do the same.

April 12, 1861 The earliest shots of the Civil
War ring out.

June 1863
Confederate forces raid
Gettysburg. Union
troops later follow, and
residents prepare for
fighting to begin.

July 1, 1863 Tillie moves in with the Weikerts,
who live on a farm south of Gettysburg.

July 1–3, 1863
Fighting occurs
in and around
Gettysburg, and the
Weikerts' property serves as a makeshift
Union hospital. Ultimately, the Union wins
the battle, though both sides suffer heavy
losses.

1871 Tillie Pierce marries Horace Alleman,
and the couple move to Selinsgrove,
Pennsylvania. They later have three
children.

1885 She begins writing a book about her
experiences during the Battle of Gettysburg.

1889 Her book is published.

March 15, 1914 She dies in Philadelphia and
is buried in Selinsgrove.

FURTHER INFORMATION

BOOKS

Donaldson, Madeline. *Deadly Bloody Battles.* Minneapolis: Lerner Publications, 2013. Take a closer look at history's bloodiest battles, including those that shaped the Civil War.

MacCarald, Clara. *The Battle of Gettysburg: Bloodiest Battle of the Civil War.* Lake Elmo, MN: North Star Editions, 2017. Explore text, illustrations, and sidebars that offer more information about the Battle of Gettysburg.

O'Connor, Jim. *What Was the Battle of Gettysburg?* New York: Grosset & Dunlap, 2013. Read about some of the key people and events that forever influenced US history.

WEBSITES

Children of the Civil War
https://www.civilwar.org/learn/articles/children-civil-war
Learn about more kids who participated in the Civil War.

Ducksters—The Battle of Gettysburg
http://www.ducksters.com/history/battle_of_gettysburg.php
Access articles, a quiz, and several links related to the Battle of Gettysburg.

Gettysburg Daily—Jacob Weikert Farm
http://www.gettysburgdaily.com/jacob-weikert-farm
Check out photos that show how the Weikerts' farm appears today.